Animal Offspring

Penguins and Their Chicks

Revised Edition

by Margaret Hall

CAPSTONE PRESS
a capstone imprint

Pebble Plus is published by Capstone Press,
1710 Roe Crest Drive,
North Mankato, Minnesota 56003
www.capstonepub.com

Library of Congress Cataloging-in-Publication Data
Names: Hall, Margaret, 1947- , author.
Title: Penguins and their chicks : a 4D book / by
Margaret Hall.
Description: Revised edition.. | North Mankato,
Minnesota : Capstone Press, 2018. | Series: Pebble plus.
Animal offspring | Includes bibliographical references
and index. | Audience: Ages 4 to 8.
Identifiers: LCCN 2017037873 (print) | LCCN 2017054337
(ebook) | ISBN 9781543508659 (eBook PDF) | ISBN
9781543508253 (hardcover) | ISBN 9781543508376 (pbk.)
Subjects: LCSH: Penguins—Infancy—Juvenile literature.
| Parental behavior in animals—Juvenile literature.
Classification: LCC QL696.S473 (ebook) | LCC QL696.
S473 H35 2018 (print) | DDC 598.4713/92—dc23
LC record available at https://lccn.loc.gov/2017037873

Editorial Credits
Gina Kammer, editor; Sarah Bennett, designer; Morgan
Walters, media researcher;
Katy LaVigne, production specialist

Photo Credits
Shutterstock: Alexey Seafarer, 5, BMJ, left 21, Brandon
B, 9, ChameleonsEye, 19, jo Crebbin, 7, niall dunne,
15, Roger Clark ARPS, Cover, 3, left 20, right 20,
StanislavBeloglazov, 11, vladsilver, 17, right 21,
Volodymyr Goinyk, 13

Note to Parents and Teachers

The Animal Offspring set supports national science
standards related to life sciences. This book describes
and illustrates penguins and their chicks. The images
support early readers in understanding the text.
The repetition of words and phrases helps early readers
learn new words. This book also introduces early
readers to subject-specific vocabulary words, which are
defined in the Glossary section. Early readers may need
assistance to read some words and to use the Table of
Contents, Glossary, Read More, Internet Sites, Critical
Thinking Questions, and Index sections of the book.

Table of Contents

Penguins

Penguins are birds that use their wings to swim. They cannot fly. Young penguins are called chicks.

5

Penguins come to land

to mate and lay eggs.

Eggs

Female penguins lay one
to three eggs. Some penguins
keep their eggs on their feet.
Other penguins keep
their eggs in a nest.

Most penguin parents take turns keeping the eggs warm.

Penguin Chicks

A penguin chick hatches from the egg. Chicks have soft feathers called down.

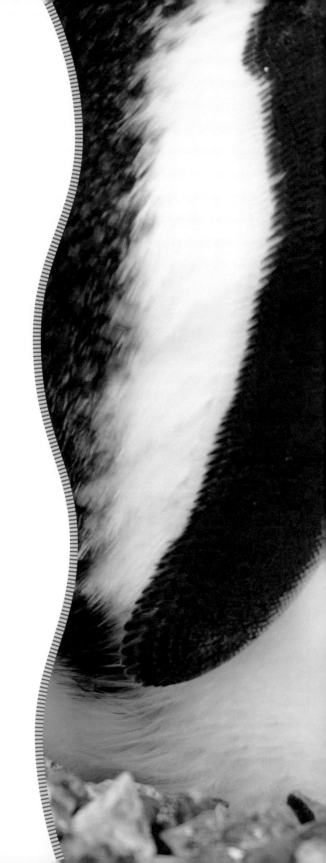

Penguin parents catch fish

for the chicks to eat.

Sometimes the chicks stand together to keep warm. Chicks grow new feathers after a few months.

Growing Up

Most penguins can swim
and take care of themselves
after about one year.

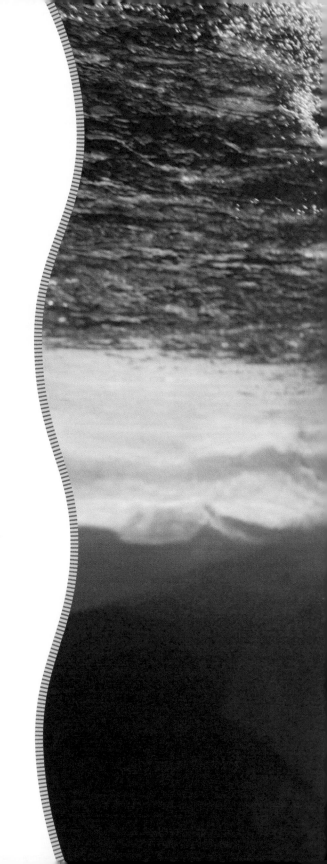

Watch Penguins Grow

adult after
about five years

21

Glossary

bird—a warm–blooded animal with wings, two legs, and feathers; birds lay eggs; most birds can fly

down—the soft feathers of a baby bird; young penguins with down cannot swim until they grow new feathers; the new feathers are waterproof

hatch—to break out of an egg; a young penguin has an egg tooth on its beak; it uses the tooth to help it break the egg open

mate—to join together to produce young; some penguins come back to the same place every year to mate

nest—a place built to raise young; some penguins make nests; other penguins keep their young warm on their feet or by using their feathers

wing—one of the feather–covered limbs of a bird; most birds move their wings to fly

Read More

Beer, Julie. *Penguins vs. Puffins.* Washington, D.C.: National Geographic Kids, 2017.

Salomon, David. *Penguins.* Step into Reading. New York: Random House Books for Young Readers, 2017.

Schuh, Mari. *Penguins.* Black and White Animals. North Mankato, Minn.: Capstone Press, 2017.

Internet Sites

Use FactHound to find Internet sites related to this book.

Visit *www.facthound.com*

Just type **9781543508253** and go.

 Check out projects, games and lots more at
www.capstonekids.com

Critical Thinking Questions

1. What does a penguin use its wings for?

2. Where can you look to find information about down feathers in this book?

3. How does standing together keep penguins warm?

Index